SUN
WHERE DO YOU GO?

By Francesca Grazzini

illustrated by Chiara Carrer

Translated by Talia Wise

A CURIOUS NELL BOOK

KM Kane/Miller Book Publishers

Brooklyn, New York & La Jolla, California

Hello Sun!
Where are you going?

Actually, I'm not
going anywhere.
I never move.
I'm always right here
in the same spot.

That can't be true; I see you rise
in the morning on one side of the world,
and then I see you set in the evening
on the other. You must go somewhere.

No, I'm telling you the truth.
The earth turns around, so
living on the earth is like
riding on a merry-go-round!
While it seems like everything
is turning around you, it's
actually you who's turning
while everything around you
is staying still.

I've never been on a
merry-go-round.
I would really like to try one.
Don't go away. Wait here for me!

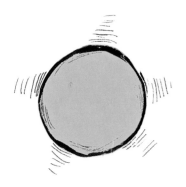

Here I am! I was on the merry-go-round. You were right!
I did think everything, even the lamp, was turning around
me, but it was the merry-go-round that was turning!
My head was spinning . . . if the earth is like a
merry-go-round, why doesn't
my head spin all the time?
Why don't I feel the earth
moving? Why don't I fall
off the earth?

There are two very important things to know about the way the earth moves. The first thing is gravity. Gravity is a force that pulls things together. The earth's gravity is what holds you down. Gravity is also what causes the second important thing; the earth's circular movement. The pull of gravity not only holds you down, but it makes the earth turn in a circle.

The earth turns slowly . . . more slowly even than a snail moves! So slowly, in fact, that you can't feel it. It takes a whole day just to make one full turn.

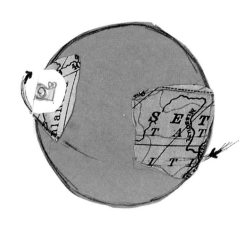

 A whole day?

 Yes! Morning, midday, afternoon, evening and night.

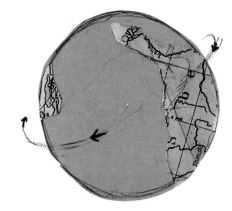

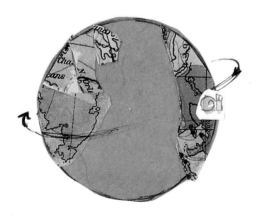

 And then?

 Then, the day begins again, because the earth never stops turning. It's been turning for billions of years. All of the other planets turn as well, some faster or more slowly than others. Their speed depends on their size, and sometimes they turn very slowly. But none of them ever stops turning.

Sun, tell me, why do
you shut yourself off at night?
Do you do this so I'll sleep well?

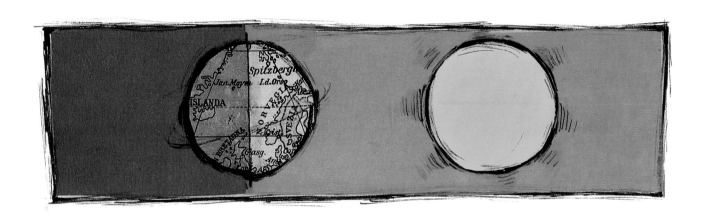

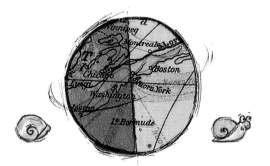

I'm not shut off. It's just that
the earth has turned around
so that the other side (the
side you're not on) is facing
me, and I give light to the
snails who live on that side.

I'm sorry you're
never around at night.
It's too bad you don't know
the moon or the stars . . . what a pity!

But I do know the moon. It's totally dark!

 Oh no, you're wrong. The moon shines!

 I shine my light on it! But it plays hide-and-seek with me, as it makes its trip around the earth. When the moon is completely behind the earth, you won't see it at all. But when it's only partially behind the earth, I can light up the part not hidden. So if only half of it is behind the earth, you'll see a half-moon; a quarter-moon if three-quarters are hidden; and so on.

FULL MOON

SETTING MOON

RISING MOON

*THE SONG OF
THE MOON*

HALF MOON

I light the night up like a lamp

It's the sun that makes me glow

My friend the sun and I play games

Like hide-and-seek, you know

But sometimes when you look for me

You may not find me there

I hide between the earth and sun

Come find me . . . if you dare!

HALF MOON

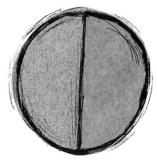

QUARTER MOON

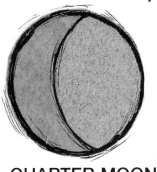

NEW MOON

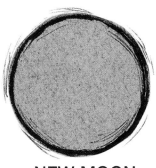

QUARTER MOON

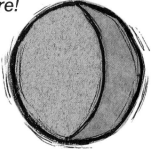

Did you know I also know the stars very well?

 How can you?

 Because I'm a star myself!

 Are you really a star?

 Yes, a star called the Sun! I look different to you because I'm so big and bright. But I only look bigger because I'm so much closer to you than the other stars. They look smaller because they are farther away. Everything looks smaller from a distance.

 Maybe there's some other star that is close to one of the other planets.

 Perhaps. It's possible that another far away sun is lighting up some other planet the way I light up the earth.

 And what would that planet be like?

 We don't know.
Maybe it has a pink sea.
Maybe extraterrestrial snails live there!

 I would like to meet an extraterrestrial snail. Who knows what it would look like!

 It would be very difficult for you to meet one.

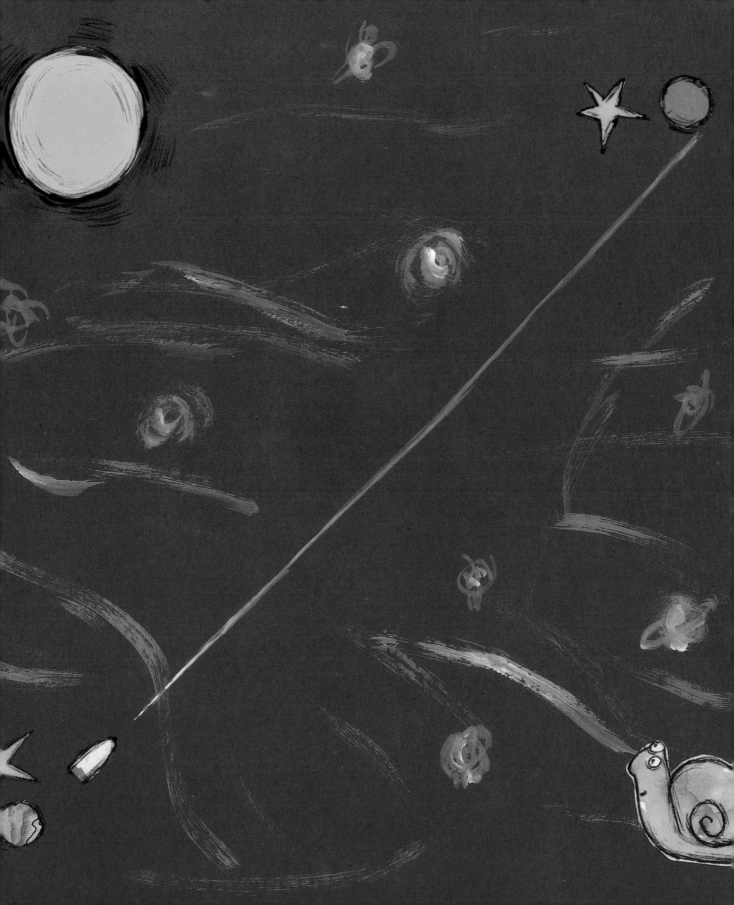

 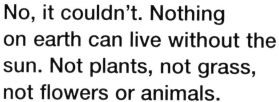

Could
another planet
like earth exist
without a sun?

No, it couldn't. Nothing
on earth can live without the
sun. Not plants, not grass,
not flowers or animals.

So we can't live without you?

No! I give light, I warm things up, I produce energy . . .

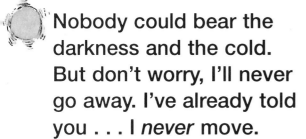 What would happen if you went away?

 Nobody could bear the darkness and the cold. But don't worry, I'll never go away. I've already told you . . . I *never* move.

Sun, but . . . in wintertime
it's cold. Why don't you
warm things up then
like in summer?

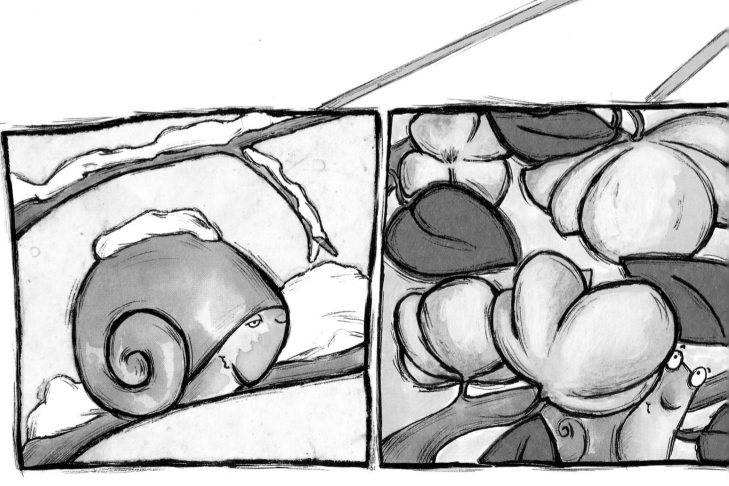

WINTER

SPRING

Because in the winter, my rays reach the earth at an angle, and aren't as strong then as when they reach the earth in a straight line. This difference is what makes the different seasons.

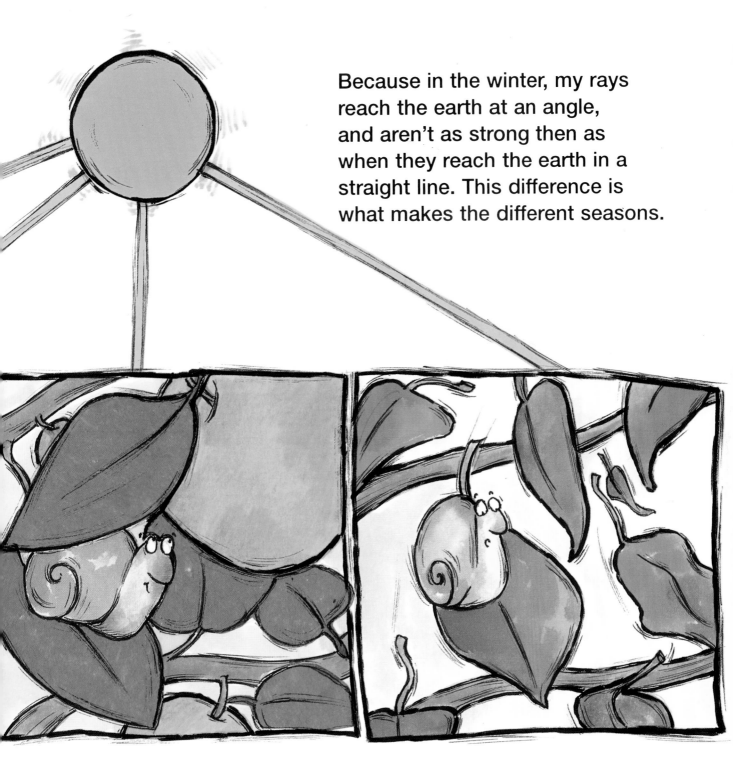

SUMMER

AUTUMN

While the earth spins a full circle every day, it's also making a full circle around me. But this circle around me takes a year, and during that time, as the angle of the earth changes and my rays hit the earth from different directions, the seasons change.

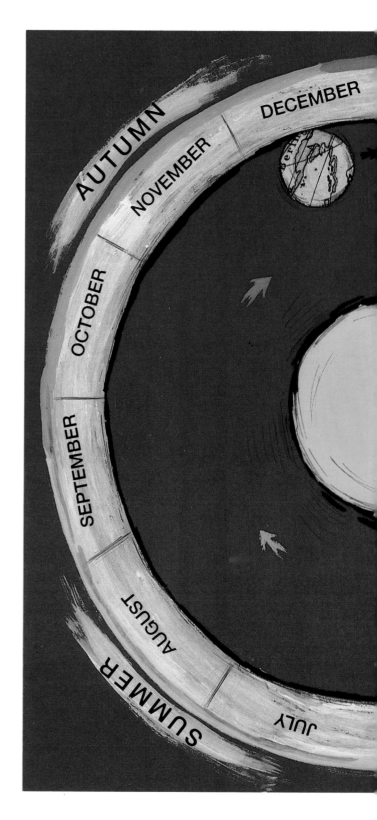

I know all this. And also that a year is made up of twelve months, and that the months are made of days, and a day lasts for twenty-four hours. So, now I'll say goodbye sun. Until tomorrow!

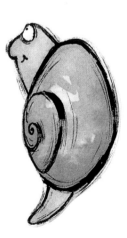

THE SUN IS A PAINTER

If the sun didn't paint
With a brush full of rays
There wouldn't be colors
On bright or dark days!

Do you want to play?
Look at the following page for
things that are the wrong color.

It's only a game . . . actually,
the sun is never wrong!

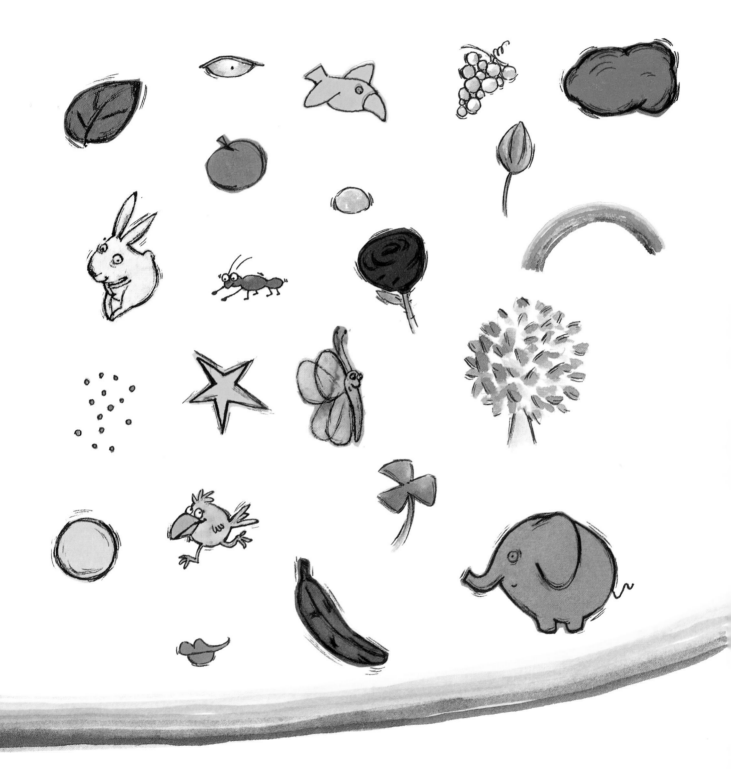

IN WHICH MONTH . . .

. . . do you try to
trick your friends?

. . . do you eat
chestnuts?

. . . do you go to
the beach?

. . . do roses bloom?

. . . do you have a
Christmas tree?

. . . do leaves fall?

. . . are there fireflies?

. . . are there
sunshowers?

. . . does ice melt?

. . . do you make
snowmen?

. . . do you celebrate
the new year?

. . . is it time to
harvest?

. . . do you carve
pumpkins?

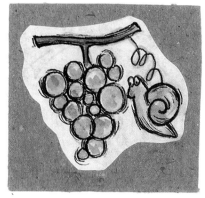

. . . is it time to
pick grapes?

. . . can you see
falling stars?